Thunderstorm

poems by

Heather Corbally Bryant

Finishing Line Press
Georgetown, Kentucky

Thunderstorm

ACKNOWLEDGMENTS

"Listening to Seamus Heaney," previously published in *Compass Rose,* Finishing
Line Press, 2016

"Calypso," previously published in *My Wedding Dress*, Finishing Line Press, 2016

"March Snow, Pine Boughs," previously published in *Compass Rose,* Finishing
Line Press, 2016

"Daylight Saving Time," previously published in *Compass Rose*, Finishing Line
Press, 2016

"Fish Ticket," previously published in *Lottery Ticket,* The University of
Wisconsin-Madison Libraries, 2013

Publisher: Leah Maines

Editor: Christen Kincaid

Cover Art: Photo used by permission of Walker B Jordan

Author Photo: Heidi Lynne

Cover Design: Elizabeth Maines McCleavy

Printed in the USA on acid-free paper.
Order online: www.finishinglinepress.com
also available on amazon.com

Author inquiries and mail orders:
Finishing Line Press
P. O. Box 1626
Georgetown, Kentucky 40324
U. S. A.

Table of Contents

For My Three Children, Who Are Each The Favorite Child

Listening to Seamus Heaney

I

The first time I heard this man read I thought I was sophisticated,
But really I was so young, a sophomore in college; I sat between my
Mother and my father; I was so busy, almost too busy to meet them
For this occasion. I remember how the words spilled forth that April
Afternoon from Heaney, the first living poet I had heard speak. I
Remember the sounds of his syllables, a poem called "Mint,"
Written after the death of his mother, the aroma of the mint she
Grew in her garden; afterwards, I told my father I wanted to be a poet;
He had been bemused, but my world had changed, I had heard a person
Explain the sorcery between the conception of an idea and a dream,
And how that magic makes a poem; I was too busy, or so I thought,
To take Heaney's course on prosody, too busy to know my own truth.

II.

As a young married woman, I heard him read for the second time
In Sanders Theatre, to a crowd filled November room; he was famous
By then, but still so humble, he explained the origins of one of his poems,
How the idea of procreation had come to him when he had peeked out
His window to see the black bag his mother's doctor
Carried with him every time just before another brother or sister
Arrived; Heaney described how he thought the baby came in
The bag, when he was supposed to be sleeping; I did not have children then,
But yearned for them, longed to be a mother; I listened to how he spoke
As both son and father. I cursed myself for not taking his course when
It was right in front of me, everything there but for the asking.

III.

Of course I read every word he wrote throughout the years, and I thought
Often of how he spoke, reminded once again alone at Harvard on a warm
October evening when the Cambridge fire brigade had to intervene
Because students filled the pathways, blocking the corridors, a hazard
To public safety. The chief fire marshal ordered half the audience
Outside where they went, disgruntled and disobliged, hanging on
The windowsills by their fingertips to hear Heaney's words floating
Through the fall evening; by then I had children, but I was already
Distrusting the contours of my life; I found his poems a comfort.

IV.

Just knowing he inhabited the universe gave me hope; so I stood
Alone in a long line waiting to have "Opened Ground" signed—he looked
Up at me after scribbling his name and said "Good luck," or "Godspeed,"
I can't remember which, and I left that room carrying the memory
Of him with me as someone who would always bear the truth of word
And soul; I reread "Mint" in the days following my own mother's
Death and I thought of how words can live forever, but not people,
Just the memory of his voice reading came alive to me; his words
Always with me; the notice of his death that August morning, close
After my own mother's, came as a shock, his voice stilled, impossible.

Calypso

Sweet Nymph and Open Sea

Meanwhile he lives and grieves upon that island
In thralldom to the nymph; he cannot stir,
Cannot fare homeward, for no ship is left him,
Fitted with oars—no crewmen or companions
To pull him on the broad back of the sea. —The Odyssey, Book V (Fitzgerald)

I saw no irony in the name of the designer who fashioned my
Wedding dress—no irony in purchasing my gown at a store
Called Calypso, also on an island—in this case, Bermuda—

It was a simple, cotton eye-lit lace mid-calf length garment—
Bought on the whirlwind of my last vacation with my parents
Before I married—we hopped a bus on a humid August noon—

In town, my father persuaded me to take a peek inside this store
Where he thought there just might be something for me—I tried
The white dress on for all of five minutes, size 6 fit me perfectly—

No alternations needed—I clutched the pink bag decorated with
Gold letters describing the goddess of temptation who persuaded
Odysseus to tarry long listening to her ambrosial songs until wiser

Heads prevailed and he set forth again on his long-delayed journey
Home where his wife Penelope was waiting for him—once he displayed
His knowledge of the trick of the bed, and his faithful dog, Argus,

Recognized him, then love was put to rights, a marriage restored,
Domestic tranquility preserved—I drew comfort from the simplicity
Of my wedding dress—it symbolized my confidence that I knew

What I was doing as I stepped down the red-carpeted aisle towards
My beaming husband-to-be, steadied by my father's arm—I believed
We loved each other with all our hearts—and so I could promise

To love for better for worse, for richer for poorer, in sickness and
In health—I believed we could sail through whatever storms life

Held in store for us—whatever journeys we undertook, it would

Be the two of us together, forever—all marriages must endure,
Sometimes less, sometimes more, if they are to last—my best
Friend tied and then retied my sash, a last minute dash to find

Something blue—a handkerchief from someone's pocket, her
Initials embroidered in turquoise—my father appeared with a
Shiny sixpence for my shoe—brought back from his last trip

To London—even though I knew he had his doubts, he granted
Me the dignity of a beautiful wedding day—there would be no
Hesitating now—we walked slowly up the stairs to wait in the

Vestibule for the trumpet voluntary to begin—he whispered
In my ear that he hoped the sixpence would bring me luck—
My father, ostensibly the least sentimental of men—offered

Me this promise of good fortune, this token with its beveled
Edges that I had tucked away in my jewelry box—just the other
Day I found it beside the pregnancy sticks that had turned blue,

Notes addressed to the tooth fairy, a purple and green bracelet
My daughter made in third grade for Mother's day—
The hospital tag I wore on my wrist the day my twins were born—

The tiny anklet identification—his own Lojack we joked—for
Our youngest son, his name and number matching mine—
For years, my wedding dress hung at the back of my closets—

As we moved from graduate student apartments and then from
House to house until one April morning when my husband told
Me he was no longer sure whether he loved me—I knew in my

Heart he was acting differently—there was a dissonance between
His words and his actions—a gap I couldn't explain as I saw the sun
Fall across his face beside our bedroom window—we were not

Where he wanted us to be, not after fifteen years of marriage then—
That was news to me—I stayed awake night after night as he flew
Around the country assuming I knew where he was and what he

Was doing—how wrong could I be—but at the time all I could think
To do was take my wedding dress to the Quality Dry Cleaners
Where I brought his shirts every week—after all, they promised

Love and memories preserved forever.

Eight years later, five hundred miles away, legally separated—I reach to
The top shelf of our cedar closet and grab the white box—I clutch the plastic
Handle to pull it down to the ground, smoothing over the pink receipt

I note the salient facts: I took the dress to the cleaners on the
Twenty-third of April, Shakespeare's birthday—I remember a clerk
Telling me that the lace had yellowed some, they would do their best

But they might not be able to make it pristine again—I said that was
Alright with me—in her rounded hand, she pressed hard and wrote
In loops: *1 wedding gown: clean and preserve*—she gave me a paper

To sign accepting the risk that it might not come entirely white
Again—even then I knew I was only trying to stem the damage—
The receipt says it would cost $110 dollars, requiring a minimum

Deposit of $75 to begin the work—the total coming to more than half
Of what the dress itself had cost—my father liked to brag that he had
Found me a beautiful wedding gown, but it had not broken the bank.

Never cheap, he did not mind finding a good bargain—my daughter
Used to wonder aloud when she looked at the pictures from our
Reception why my dress had not had a train, why it had been so plain—

She was sure, even at seven years of age, that she would want a
Fancier wedding than her father and I had—I think it is safe to
Assume she will not want to wear my dress—nor, I think, would I

Have wanted her to—twenty three and a half years later, I haul
The white box containing my wedding dress to the Saint Vincent
De Paul store where I hope it may give another woman a chance

At happiness—after I drive away from leaving the box just inside
The door, plastic handle still intact—I return home in the rain only
To have my husband call to ask if he can move back in again—

I know then the only answer I can give to his question.
I also know that I have no earthly idea where I am going—
My landscape terrifying—I awake dreaming I'm drowning.

The Barn

Although I wish I could say I did not, I have
Some small idea of the despair that led this
Beautiful woman, mother and wife, to walk

Out to the barn when no one else was there—
I have some fragmentary understanding of
The idea that all is lost—as I felt when I dialed

A suicide hotline on Labor Day weekend, my
Husband was calling me from another woman's
Apartment across the country; they'd just come

Back from grocery shopping, they were about
To prepare and then share a lovely meal together;
I stood in our bathroom, a complete cliché, home

With three teenagers, trying to keep the life we'd
Built for a quarter century swirling around me—
And the whole weekend felt more than crazy;

I bought a hair dryer, attended a track meet,
Entertained friends who wondered aloud just
Who it was who would have to work on a long

Weekend—everything mocked me, and by the
Miserable end I was sitting in an attorney's
Office with very little idea of the storm that lay

Ahead of me, simply with the knowledge that
There was a part of me wanting to be dead—
Her husband, as did mine, said that she was

Crazy, that she leapt out of the car as he tried
To restrain her and take her to a place where
She could be helped, where other people could

Cure what ailed her—she drank too much, drove

Recklessly, it was not safe for her children to stay
With her—he had to leave, and yet no one else

Was around when he said these things; she grabbed
His arm, he had to restrain her; there was no one
To hear his accusations, his insinuations, maybe

He had also told her once that he would never leave
Her, that he loved her more than life itself, that he
Would do anything for her, she had borne his

Children—he says now there was nothing anyone
Near her didn't do, couldn't do for her—his protests
Make me wonder just a little bit why he was so busy

Talking, why he was so busy gallivanting with another
Woman, while the woman he said he once loved
Endured so much more than any one person should

Have to—it is never easy to say who knew what or where
Or when love stopped, or if it could ever begin again—
But there she was, left alone in the house they had built

Together, where they had made their family and yet,
Not—she knew it could vanish in a second and while I
Wish I do not, I have some small understanding of what

Might have been running through this woman's mind
As she walked out to the barn she built that probably
Smelled sweet, of horses and love and warmth and all

The childhood afternoons when she thought she was
Making love with her husband while he was busy falling
Into the arms of another woman and using his money

And power to threaten her, to rebuke her, to announce
That he would take everything away from her, leaving

Not one last thing, not even the children she had birthed.

While I wish I do not, I have some small understanding
Of what this woman might have been thinking or feeling
As she walked out alone, when no one else was home,

To find a final escape from the walls that were collapsing
In upon her—it must have been very quiet and still and
Also more sorrowful than anyone else can ever know—

What it might have been like inside a tormented soul—
But then we come to the chicken and egg question—did
She begin her life that way, or did someone make her that

Way after a lifetime of yearning for love from the man who
Had promised to love her forever—did that make her into
A woman she did not wish to become—someone who,

When presented with the loss of everything—someone
Who had to make an exit from this place she could no
Longer bear, no one to help her except for the very man

Who could not stop hurting her—I wish I did not have to
Know what it would be like not to want to make it through
One more night, when the man who promised to love me

Forever and ever began to look the other way all the while
Insisting that it was only I who was crazy—if only I could
Have been thinner, richer, smarter, quicker, more like

Whatever woman happened to walk by next—if only I could
Have been more like them then he would not have been so
Unable to prevent himself from straying—if only I could have

Looked the other way while he followed his desire—I am
Filled with sorrow for this woman who could not stop walking
Towards the barn, who could not stay her desire to stop her

Own breathing, and I know now why she could not turn the other
Way—I am filled with tenuous gratitude that I was able to
Make it through another night, that I was able to stand up to

My husband and say I will not allow you to prevent me from
Making it through another day, for staying here on earth.

March Snow, Pine Boughs

The bared circle of ground, a shovel stuck in snow, a mound of dirt—
Suddenly it was all too much for me—I had been thinking of how warm
My mother's body had been as I lay beside her long after she had stopped

Breathing; her fever had been so high her cheeks were still pink, her flesh
Soft as I watched her quilted body being wheeled down the hall to, of all
Things, a minivan, that I had not expected; the undertaker slipped the black

Bag into the back while her nurse stood by to see her patient off to the
Crematorium. She folded the blue quilt silently, then put her arm around
Me as we walked back inside, I could see her cheeks glistening with tears.

Almost two months later, I stood with my children and our friends to bury
The pine box containing her ashes; it had been impossible for me to imagine
How tiny the container would be, how all that my mother had been, and all

That she would be, had been distilled to ash and bone; I never wanted to
Touch her more than at that moment; the minister asked me if I had any
Last words to say and I could not think of a single one; I rushed back to the

Car, my black heels skidding on the snowy, muddy ground, and grabbed my
Note, the envelope with pictures of her grandchildren, and I reached
Down to place the letter among pine boughs, yellow tulips, rough dirt.

Daylight Saving Time

Optimist that my mother was, at least most of the time, she always
Waited for this season—in fact, she began waiting for it the moment
She saw the days getting shorter—she would say, everyday now,
Everyday, the light will be getting longer; on this first time without her,

We turn the clocks back, it so happened to be that was the day I chose
For her service—she would have loved that, I do know—she would
Have liked nothing better than to see how the light flowed through the
Purple windows of the Memorial Church on that sunny Sunday afternoon

In March, the month of her birth, also by chance St. Patrick's Day—
How I wish I could turn to her and say, "See, the days are getting longer,
Isn't that great?" And I imagine her turning back to me and saying,
"How I wish I were still alive to see the weeping willows greening."

Sky

Just by the way she was sitting the doctor could tell she was in an abusive
Relationship—seven years later—she sees the same doctor again

And she thanks him—he is not shocked—at the time she was blind, blind to
What she would not see, but now she knows what he saw in her then, just

By the way she was sitting, just by the look in her eye, a hunted haunted look
Was what he called it, like a dog who is accustomed to being hit.

Carpet Dreams

I associate planting petunias on Memorial Day weekend with my dad, funny
Really because I can't think of anyone who liked to garden less—he had a habit
Of disappearing when my mom said anything about weeding or

Hoeing—not so odd, really for a man who loved to take care of people, books,
And libraries—he had no patience for shoveling or raking—yet, I always find
Myself planting something on this holiday that

Is suffused with memories of him—it was on this weekend during the last
Couple months of his life that he told me how much trouble he was having
Breathing, on this weekend that I began understand how soon he might be

Leaving and I remember filling the window boxes on our first porch with purple
Petunias before dashing in to the hospital to see him one more time—always
One more time—it never seemed there would be a last time

Until there was—he died on June 12th, just a few days before his birthday and I
Was surprised at the small flag placed beside his burial ground—he always
Dismissed his military service in World War Two as only a desk job—

As I grew older, I wondered more about what he was doing first in Washington,
Then London, then Berlin after the war—I wish I had asked him more about
What it meant to be special attaché for the US embassy—

Whenever I asked him if he'd been a spy, he always gave the same wry answer:
"You know I cannot say,"—and I think of him now and how much I would give
To be able to talk to him again, to hear the sound of his voice, to listen

To the dreams he had for me, to tell him about the dreams his grandchildren
Are fulfilling—today, as I gathered up the plastic containers still filled with dirt,
I read aloud the apt name of the petunias I'd chosen: "Carpet Dreams."

The Cafe

Everyday I came to this cafe, every morning, first thing, when the light awakened
Me I walked down the cobbled streets, keeping out of the donkey's way—first
Thing, I came to this place and drank one cappuccino—

Sometimes two—and I felt everything again, as if for the first time—I could see
All the way to the horizon's line, I could feel my world righting itself again—I
Stopped waking feeling as though I were falling, falling through

Everything until there was nowhere left to fall—on this magical island I began
To believe I could live again in beauty and in peace, as though I could imagine a
New universe where there was more sunshine and less grief—

Every morning, the proprietor brought me two pastries with my drink—
Everyday we greeted one another with grins; when I put my coins on the
Counter, he wished me good day, and on my very last morning he waived

The receipt away and wished me Godspeed on my trip home to England—I
Pretended that's where I lived—in our two weeks, we had learned so little about
One another and yet, if I saw him tomorrow, I would smile at him.

When I First Came Here

For my first three weeks in central Pennsylvania, the sun did not shine, not
Once—the mountains I had glimpsed one azure September day had slipped
Behind clouds of opacity—the sky had dulled, dimmed—I could no longer

See my own shadow, not even enough to be afraid of it—I gathered the courage
To call the one person I knew here, my first friend, and ask her when the sun
Might come out again—she was tactful yet honest—it was,

She said, typical for this time of winter, for January, to be cloudy—I began to
Long for yellow rays, for anything to distinguish the dull and gloomy days, one
From the other—I began to wonder if I had imagined the mountains

After all—and then, spring came, the skies cleared—and eventually, I moved
Across town to where I could see the horizon, even on a gray morning—and
Sometimes, now, I awaken in a moment of summer mist as if

I lived among the clouds—whispers of them waft through my view across
Farmer's fields, across telephone poles, across ridges of Mount Tussey, places
Where the folded edges of the land sometimes catch the sunshine.

Sometimes A Cliché Is Not a Cliché

Sometimes a cliché is not a cliché, as in today when I passed not one, but two
Families of ducklings hatched—the first set, the older ones followed their mom
When they heard my footsteps—to hightail it across the lawn—

But I did not dare to photograph the other crew, the mother was huddling over
Her two remaining ducklings, as though she needed to protect them especially
Against whatever threat, like me, who might come near—and in

This tender season of endings and beginnings, of graduations and births, I
Remember what it was like to hold my babies all day long, as I did on many
May afternoons when holding them was all it seemed I could do—now

They are almost grown—and I cherish this stage too, where everything is
Unfolding and we can laugh about when they were brand new and I had so
Little clue about what to do—now I know it is time to let them go—time to

Let them cross the asphalt to see what is on the other side, letting them know I
Am here, waiting, to hear what they have to say, listen to where they want to go,
What they want to do, letting them be who they already are.

Moccasin Flower, or Lady Slipper

These soft tuber flowers have acquired substantial meaning in my life—like
Yeats's Tower, or Stevens' jar—they have become both signifier and metaphor—
Not so distant cousins of the orchid family, these pink bulbs

Have appeared as balms at crucial junctures through the years, seemingly out
Of the blue—on one particularly sad May day, I was walking alongside a friend
In the place I used to live—when she stopped and smoothed away

The brown leaves to show me the tenderness of the pale purple blossom—more
Than a decade later, on a trail in Tennessee, or North Carolina, wherever the
Exact border may be—a whole grove of them

Sheltered under an old oak tree; some legends say these flowers contain
Magical properties, definitely medicinal ones—the roots were long believed to
Cure nervousness, tooth pain, and muscle spasms—also held as good

Remedies for nervousness or anxiety—as a child, I remember my mother
Pulling my hand away from a tuber, reprimanding me for thinking I could pick
These petals to keep; she said they were too special to pluck—just as

Cinderella's sleek glass slipper remained her only trapping as a princess, the
Only way her prince could find her, the only signifier of her identity, the only
Way she could be seen for the beauty she always would be.

Wildflowers: the Names

I've never been good at remembering the names of the flowers—or even at
Distinguishing between blossom and imposter, between what should

Remain in the garden and what no longer belongs there—I already forget what
These corn silk flowers are called, maybe blue bonnets or violets,

At least I know what they are not: lupines—when I was a child, I thought
Lupines held mystical properties, or so I liked to believe—I no longer recall

Whether the lupines in our garden changed color every year, like chameleons,
Or whether I just made up that story because I liked the idea—

Daydreaming about lupines certainly beat weeding—I can still recite a few
Names of the flowers from northern New England—larkspur, loosestrife,

Lupine, Queen Anne's lace, quilted beds of lilies of the valley spreading cloying
Sweetness everywhere, white bells blossoming, softening our

Footfalls one May noontime when we are far from the place we call home.

Fish Ticket

If you catch one of them crabs
With orange on its claw, you'll get
A fish ticket, says the six-year-old
Boy filled with wisdom standing
On the edge of the Frisco pier—

Down the way, a big man catches
One Sheep Head after another, piling
The Black and White zebra stripes
One by one—our rods baited with
Smaller pieces of worm—we cast
Yellow lines out—
Looking for a Spot, a Gray Trout,
Maybe a Bluefish if we're lucky.

Fish by fish, the string begins to
Tighten—and we reel them in,
Unhook them, careful for the blood
And toss them out into the sunset
Waters—

Just before dark, we catch one last
Baby Spot—*Can I have it for bait?*
And sweetly, you hand it over to the
Little boy who seems to have come
Here alone—a grin of thanks is
Enough for the customs of this place.

The Tea Bag

An autumn morning, Paris, a tea bag placed in my silver pot—
Madame, the waiter rushed over from across the room—
He cried out again, *Madame,* my French lapsed, I could
Not understand this man—clearly, I had done something

Wrong, offended his sensibility—but it was early, I was
Jet lagged after flying across the ocean—our room not
Yet ready—*Madame*—this time he was imploring me to
Do something—I raised my arms in frustration—and he

Gestured one more time—finally, I got it, the penny
Dropped—I had not allowed the tea to steep long enough
In the hot water—I nodded—with care, I plucked the bag
And set it back in the silver pot—the waiter smiled a bit

Before he retreated—in America, I thought, no one
Would care how strong or weak my tea was to drink.

Night Daffodil

Emily Dickinson gardened only at night, or so they say, always wearing all
White—I remember—as I take the dog out for a stroll on this luminescent
April Evening,

I pass one yellow daffodil and I think of the quiet house on the quiet street
Where the poet wrote and wrote, where she sewed packets for her poems

To keep in her bureau drawers, where she kept them safe, away from light, away
From both criticism but also praise, where she lived out her days in

Solitude—it's a strange thing, really, when you decide you want to let the light
Shine on your words—I have a closet full of scribblings in notebooks,

So many notebooks that the shelves sag—and one day I decided I wanted to let
The sunlight in again, I wanted to remember what I saw and felt each

Day—I wanted to see what, if anything, I had to say—I wanted to perceive
Everything in front of me with richness and delight, only in full sunlight.

Double Yolks

I crack open one extra large egg, purchased from the local farm, just down the
Road from me, where we see the cows eating grass, chewing,

Wandering, returning to be milked in the evenings—a double yolk slips from
The shell, like twins, two for one, one and then the second one, and I

Recall my joy on that blistering last day of June when I learned there would be
Not one but two babies, known to me then only as baby a and baby b,

How quickly they would both slip out of me, arriving long before they were due
Surprising me at noon, just as they have every day since then, eight

Long minutes separating my son from my daughter—my father used to call
Double yolks lucky when he tapped eggs against the frying pan with his

Steady hand—when he let them sizzle sunny side up just for me, squishy.

This Vehicle Has Been Checked for Sleeping Children

Today I sat in a traffic jam behind a yellow school bus, the small kind for
Kindergartners—and because the light was long, I had a lot of time to study the
Back of the bus—I got close enough to read the handwritten sign taped

Inside the back window: "This Vehicle has been checked for sleeping Children,"
And I thought about what those words meant, and why they had to be there at
All, in the first place—and then I realized how many children

I have read about who end up left on buses, or sent to the wrong town—and I
Thought again about randomness, about the panic of a parent who realizes a
Child has gone missing—and the terror accompanying those moments of

Anticipated or imagined loss—how our hearts immediately start pounding—
How we are wired to know where are children are, to know they are as safe as is
Humanly possible—and I thought about how very big the

World is, and how small each one of us really is, and what a miracle it is that
Any one of us is here at all, in the first place—when the glistening cells begin to
Grow within us, or when we gather up another woman's child into

Our arms, loving a baby into our life, that is where the beauty comes, in knowing
That love can be made flesh, and that flesh can be loved forever and ever, no
Matter the beginning, village, city, country, world, universe.

Rolling the Dice

By the time my mom knew about my upcoming poetry collection, *Lottery Ticket*, she had just started on oxygen full-time; a friend told me he thought she Probably had about six months left—and he was right, almost,

Short by just two months. she surprised us all by living longer than any of us Thought she might—and, until the very end, she never lost her sharp wit, her Inquisitive nature. She made no secret about her puzzlement at my title:

"But you've never bought a lottery ticket, have you?" I could look in her eyes And say I had not; she did not approve of gambling—her own mother had been An inveterate purchaser of scratch tickets—and every now and then

Had won a small sum. "No, I said, I have not." I could see my mom, she Was always thinking—even when she was confused, she was still thinking— Sometimes I thought I could hear her thinking. "So why did

You call your book that then?" Stymied, as I often was with her, I hesitated; I Wanted to explain about how I had been thinking about the randomness of life, Of the luck involved beginning with the accident of our birth. She and I

Were sitting at lunch together on a warm October Sunday afternoon—I had Persuaded her to leave her room—she was self-conscious about her oxygen— She did not want to need it, as she did—and there we were, eating

Lobster salad, a mutual favorite—when she looked up at me and said, "I know, You meant marriage." It was my turn to furrow my brow—I paused, if I

Waited I had a better chance that she might tell me what she was thinking: "What do you mean?" She answered, cogent and pithy as always, "Marriage, Is always a lottery ticket." Then, she smiled with a faraway look in her eyes:

"Don't you worry, honey," she said in comfort, "You just didn't win yet."

My Mail

My mail these days is strange, bills from my mother's cancer diagnosis, her last
hospital stay where she received her final sentence before her doctors sent her
home to die, but told her she should enjoy every last day, her issues of the *New
Yorker* I don't have the heart to cancel yet, notices of her generosity of spirit—it
seems, at least, as though she gave money to every cause: disabled veterans,
six food banks, centers for women's health, political causes right and left, for a
woman of her age she was remarkably progressive—every time I see her name
on an envelope at my address I remember that she is no longer here, not now,
nor ever will she be again and I miss her; I walk past the bench beside the
graduate commons where I sat one sunny noon last September and listened to
her tell me with clarity and will that all she had left to do was to die; the thing
she was most afraid of, death, had come to challenge her and there was nothing
for any of us to do except to wait for her to take her very last breath; I did
everything in my power to be there at the end, to hold her while she began her
journey to somewhere far away, somewhere where I can no longer see her, nor
hear her voice, unless I listen to her last garbled message calling out for me to
free her; perhaps what I miss most of all is just the knowledge that she is near,
that I could call her to tell her the weather here is warm.

Air

The air is thinner here—we breathe in deeply, gazing at mountains over mist—
And air is here with us, always air—we speak of the Smokey's, of living simply
Here, now—my babies were almost born not knowing how to

Breathe, their lungs weren't ready, so the doctor said, and he injected me twice
With a potent drug which hastened their breaths; at birth, they breathed on their
Own, and I listened and watched the monitors, the green

Lines blipping steadily along, until they would dip and I would jostle their chests
To remind them to breathe—I was so grateful to see their ribs move, I marvel at
What I took then as my new reality, reminding my children's

Bodies to breathe—that seems another life now, another scene and it was—
Today I saw an elderly man leaning on a railing, catching his oxygen from a
Cart—and I remembered how my mom fought the oxygen, told the nurses she

Was fine without it—the canister annoyed her, got in the way of what she wanted
To be doing; I got it—no one wants to have to need help breathing for, in the end,
That is the essence of what we are—of here, and now, of air, pushing in out and

Of our lungs—lately, I have been finding it is helpful to think only of my breath,
Only flowing in and out of my body, in and out, so it is our most primal and
Essential practice: the last to leave us, the first to bring us into this remarkable

And joyous world, so easy to forget what allows us to begin and to end.

The Road to Nowhere, Swain County

I suspect every one of us has, at one time or another, found ourselves on what
Feels like a road to nowhere—a dead end job, a failed love affair, a dispiriting
Time for one reason or the other—but here, in Bryson City,

North Carolina there really is a road to nowhere—the government took land
Away from people who had lived there forever, along highway 288—
Promises were made—Lakeview Drive was going to be newer,

Better as it would swoop along the shores of manmade Fontana Lake—instead,
Chaos erupted as humans tried yet again to bend nature toward our will—and
Now the old highway is buried under the lake and the

Road to nowhere comes to an abrupt end at a half moon tunnel shaped out of
Stone—that is the state of affairs—on summer weekends, families can take
Ferries out to see the cemeteries where their ancestors are buried—

As I drove along this road last week and looked out over this winding lake, I
Thought about how we take and how we give, and how we often confuse giving
For taking; it is much easier, and kinder never to forget how to give.

Lavender

The first year I planted lavender and Black-Eyed Susans beside it—but only
The Lavender survived—bees loved it, and they swarmed blossoms in early
Mornings and late afternoons—in Provence, a friend's daughter cried when

She was stung for the first time, just as my daughter had cried the first time she
Was stung when she was five—and all I could do was give her Benadryl and
A paste to soothe her smarting forehead—she wanted me to swear

She would never be stung again—and then told me she probably would never
Go outside If she heard a bee buzzing—it was an early stark lesson in knowing I
Could not promise always to keep her safe—in France, last

Summer, the fast train blew along the countryside, past miles and miles of
Lavender and Goldenrod, planted side by side, yellow and purple—briefly, I
Thought of bringing a sachet of dried lavender back for my mom—she used

To slip them between the sheets in the linen closet—and when she pulled them
Out, they smelled soft and sweet— but then I remembered all over again that
She was dead—still, when I smell lavender, I think of her—and

Now when I walk out my front door past the June blooms, I miss her anew.

The Red Dress

Because I knew for five months that my mom was dying, and because I knew
She had been, as her doctor said, "given," six months at most to live, I kept
Buying black dresses; it was almost unconscious. I would find myself

Browsing the blacks in all my local stores—by the end, I had at least six to
Choose from, and yet, that March morning of her service, I still couldn't decide
Which one to wear—I picked one from years ago, one which felt

Familiar and had some sparkles so it was not as bland as the funereal ones I
Had planned. After she died, I kept buying dresses, but only the brightest ones
I could find—more dresses than I could ever wear—and only in garish

Hues I usually did not hang in my closet—pinks, oranges, yellows, reds,
Fuchsias, cranberries, purples, turquoises, a few beiges, baby blues, roses,
Lots of greens, her favorite color, from emerald to

Sprouts of grass just starting to take seed. In the year following her death, I
Bought more clothes than I had in my entire life—I bought cardigans, blouses,
Scarves—I wanted everything that touched my skin to

Feel soft, warm, comforting—I wore her pearls everyday until I twirled them
So many times the strand frayed—a psychologist once told me that is not an
Entirely uncommon reaction to the loss of a mother's familiar encircling arms.

Before

She didn't know the tenderness of a man's touch—she didn't know how much
She had been missing—she didn't know she could say the truth when she

Felt mad or blue—she didn't know she could long for his body, she had
No idea of how it could feel to lie next to him in the warm afterglow of love—in

High school she learned to conjugate the verb: amo, amas, amat

But that told her nothing about what love means and how that word must
Be savored, treasured, cherished, most of all nourished, told her nothing

About how silly love could be, how love could make her laugh, make her feel
Beautiful, and free—before she met him she had no idea how to love a man.

On Not Writing a Poem

Yesterday I didn't write a poem—words and images flowed through my mind
But I could never get them quite aligned—I saw myself floating—
A toddler smelling a rose, as a young mother carrying

My babies, as a lover, as a teacher, as a daughter, as a scholar, as once a wife
But now a wanderer—and time seemed to elongate and then snap closed, just
As soon as I tried to grab a word or phrase, it eluded me—leaving me

Disorganized, mistrustful—as though this gift of words could flee at any
Moment—before a thought could elapse another one came in—until I could no
Longer remember where one word or world ends and where I begin.

Camera Obscura

I still remember the lecture hall where I was sitting on a late April day, almost
Into May, where I first heard that the position of the observer determines
The outcome of the experiment—all my life until then

I had wondered how different people could see the same thing so differently—
And that, I suppose, is why I am always writing, always trying to figure out
What it is that I see, and what it is that others see, and where

Middle ground can be found—everything, really comes back to how we see
And what we do with what we see—for so long I lived with a mystery inside my
Own life, a secret that made no sense to me—I spent years unraveling

What I could not believe—and when the time came for me to open my eyes
I saw a painful, raw truth—for the first time I realized that it takes much more
Bravery to look at what terrifies us, to accept the random

Nature of our universe, so much harder to use the free will given to us, if we so
Choose to use it, then we can do anything—it is only a matter of accepting the
Gift of choice, coupled with the burden of randomness—

So much easier to live a life in the light, no longer hiding in darkness.

Somewhere on a Dark Road

Somewhere on a dark road a man is driving—it is raining and car beams
Tunnel the lights—she remembers the first time he told her he liked her—
No one had ever said those words to her that way, not in the way that he did

Later, he told her they had never been out of one another's lives—and, looking
Back, she realized that was true—those words were new to her, the idea also,
The love, the kindness, the understanding—so when she thinks of him driving

Far away on that dark road in the middle of a nowhere she does not know, she
Thinks of the light he has brought into her life, the hope, the laughter, the
Recognition of what a man and a woman can be together—somewhere in the

Middle of the night, somewhere on a dark road, a feeling stirs in my heart.

Vermont, Queen Anne's Lace

These leafy spindly flowers fly by us, or do we fly by them on our way to where
And when—these flowers always remind me of lattices, or cornices, secret
Places where we would gather them by handfuls on a summer

Vermont afternoon, where we would braid them together and wear them as
Crowns, queens of our own worlds long ago then when we dreamed of who we
Would become and how—on those sunny July afternoons when we

Jumped in the lake and washed our hair with Herbal Essence shampoo and
What did we know then, so little really, of all that life could be—those camping
trips Where our lives were suspended between beginning and end

And we were practicing to become who we now are—and these winding roads
Remind me of what has been lost, but more, what has been gained—as I still
Gather with those friends and remember bonfires,

Marshmallows, Sunday blueberry pancakes on the hill, sweetened with syrup
From Vermont maples, perhaps coming from the same places where our
Laundry was steamed, made clean— these white flowers remind me of

Chastity long ago, boys kissed, wishes made—some coming true in the blue of
A Vermont summer afternoon—when we looked upon grownups with their
Annoying slowness, their deliberateness of pace—for us, it was all

About the chase, about who we were right then, and how the world opened
Before us as I read *Ulysses* on a green lawn of a day off—or when we drove
Around the lake to have a few drinks at the inn, our laughter echoing

Back at us, at the fuss we made over nothing, at the sweetness of oranges when
We went climbing, of the simplicity of choice of peanut butter and jelly or
Salami—how we waited for the dance with the boys on the fourth

Of July—of how sweet it was to wake to reveille, to sleep at taps, to rest in the
Afternoons, to lick stamps on postcards that we wrote to our city friends, how
We stood in line to put our hot and sticky hands on the black

Payphone hanging on the wall, how we had to whisper across the lines—of how

Quickly the time passed, so little time for chat—we were, by force of nature in
The here and now—and that was how our days went, our time

Spent, impossible to explain to anyone who had not been there then—the
Queen Anne's Lace, how we toppled their blossoms and pretended we liked
To eat them, their sweetness like the carrots we might feed to

Horses—how we swam across the lake and back, how I learned the perfect dive,
How July seeded into August and then the flowers were blowing away in the
Soft winds—and how we didn't want them ever to stop blooming—

We pressed them between the pages of our special notebooks, just for us—at
Home, months later, we could open the books and smell the summer all over
Again—how a boy I knew drove all the way from Washington, DC to see

Me—how I had to sneak back up to my tent, the dew already wet with morning—
How I baked clay, ran, laughed, and sailed—how I sat on wooden logs set into
The hillside and prayed, though I didn't know why or for

What—all this comes rushing back as the flowers pass by in a flash—eight
Weeks could be so long—and then gone again, all of us standing in a circle,
Crying our goodbyes, knowing how long summer could take to come—and

All this I remember driving along these windy mountain passes with names
Like Queechee and White River Junction, how rarely we drove, how we parceled
Out our free time and sat on the lawn making crowns out of the

Lace—we know less than we thought, but perhaps more than I knew now as
I think of life flying by like a summer afternoon that has simply ended too
Soon—one quick jump in the lake, one more memory to make, one more

Bouquet of flowers to gather, to remember everything, everything matters.

The Sixth Month

In June so many lives have folded and unfolded inside me—once on the last day
Of the month—I heard I was carrying twins, in the doctor's words I was, "Very,
Very pregnant," until then, I did not know a woman could be more or

Less pregnant—I thought you either were or were not—but then, life
Is other than I thought—I did not know that "until death do us part" would not
Be a part of my story—in June, the rhododendrons bloom—pink

And purple extravaganzas exploding everywhere—my father would take me to
See the largest bank near our house and we would admire them together—then
I thought he was fussing over nothing—now I understand

The apparent glory in June, in those early days of spring, when we wish for
Everything—another spring has come and that spring, inherently leads us to
Think of what has begun and also what has come undone—what has

Been woven and what has been untied—as all our lives coincide—in June I had
A strange metallic taste in my mouth during the early days of my pregnancy—
All I wanted to drink was tomato juice, small cans of it lined

The kitchen counter; I couldn't bear to see naked chicken breasts, or even catch
A whiff of pizza baking—in June, we always celebrated my father's birthday,
Once in London with a store-boughten cake, as he would have

Dubbed it—another time he faked gladness for the muddle I had baked with
No liquids because I was too stubborn to ask for help with the recipe—in June
The rhododendrons bloom—in June, my father died—on the twelfth

Day of the sixth month of the year, confirming my mother's superstition that
People often die near their births—my grandmother used to call the twelfth of
June a bad luck day, Her own wedding day—her husband had

Died young, just before his own thirtieth birthday—in June, we buried
My father's ashes—I let the soft flakes pass through my hands as I tried to
Make myself understand he was gone—in June, he would say, in June the
Rhododendrons will

Bloom—and there was comfort in hearing those words, comfort in knowing he

Was still here, comfort in remembering how he would stand and gesture at the
Beauty—in June I finally was able to tell him he would be a grandfather

In June I said that, if I had a son, he would be named for him—my father's smile
Was worth everything to me—in June, on the last night he was conscious—I sat
With him and watched the sun set over the Charles River through his hospital

Room—in June, he told me I would be alright, even as he said those words I
Knew he would not make it through the night—in June, we gathered his ashes
Together and buried him beneath the Chinese dogwood that was in full bloom,

The kind of tree he loved—that June, it was still a sapling—now it is full-grown,
Almost overgrown, shading the earth where he is buried. In June beginnings
And endings come to pass as we each remember again how it feels to be so alive

After all those months of dormancy—in June, we begin—in June the petunias
Bloom and we smell the sweet lilies, we watch the roses burst into flower, we
Watch the magnolias begin to lose their soft white, pink, and yellow petals.

We whisper in prayer beauty after darkness, the promise of life after death.

Currents

For my eldest son

When I was pregnant with you, I loved to swim at the beginning—it was like
Being suspended between my body and the water, currents trickling—

I was so surprised the first time I felt you move—it was early September and the
Ocean was still warm—someone told me I would know the second I

Felt you—I thought it would be something momentous, earth-shattering—but
As with so many other instants in life, it was not anything

Like what I had imagined—at first I wasn't even sure what I was feeling, I was
Not clear about what came over me that Thursday, it started, startlingly

Like being tickled, almost as though a butterfly was fluttering inside me—as I
Walked into the water that first autumn afternoon, perhaps just past a

Full moon, I balanced myself on the waves—feeling water all around me, also
Inside me, and I understood why I had seen other women rubbing

Their bellies—and I giggled with joy that you were alive already, steadily
Growing and becoming you—these many years later I can still count on you

To be present, kind, keeping others in mind as you tower above me now, you
Still show me the way, reminding me always of what is essential: to be here.

Somersaults

For my daughter

Perhaps it should not surprise me that you are a swimmer—it seems natural,
Inevitable that you should feel so at home in the water—I think of your watery
Beginnings, of the very first days when you were an embryo, and then a flutter,
And then a person who

Always hid behind your brother—you were always moving, born moving, but
Gracefully—the first time I took you to the ocean you cried at the noise the
Waves made—you were terrified when you saw high tide, the water rolling in
Close—but from

The moment you entered the water on your own, you never wanted to get out
Again—I would have to pull you from the pool—fingers pruned and water-
Logged—and wrap you in a towel—each time you cried because you didn't
Want to leave—and I remember how

Determined you were to beat me as we raced laps together—and it did not take
You long, not long at all, before you were way faster than me, at the ready—
From the first dive—you said the water made you feel alive—and when I watch
You swim now I picture your

Smile, the kind of smile that says everything without a word, and I remember
The winter night, shortly before your early birth, when you flipped inside
Me and turned yourself right side down, feet first, saving us all from a very
Complicated birth—I cannot put

Into words what it felt like to have you do a somersault inside my belly—when
You turned, the book I was reading fell on the floor—I had a feeling then, and it
Was only a feeling—that you would be quite something when you were born—
And for these fast

Twenty years you have showed me everyday just how quite something you are.

Flame Orange

In the Appalachian mountains, these flame orange azaleas grow spontaneously,
A rarity considering they are a "naturally occurring Tetraploid" meaning they
Possess two times as many chromosomes as the

Surrounding native flora—their rarity makes for their beauty—their neon
Brightness lights up an entire hillside, bright stars of color etching glory side by
Side—and seeing them makes me think about the wonder of our species,

Both natural and unnatural, and I remember just how many sequences of DNA it
Takes to make a baby, a preoccupation of mine for a very long time—and I am
Reminded all over again, of just how lucky any single one of

Us is to be here at all, for however long we are given, we need to keep looking
For the orange blossoms hidden among the brambles and overgrowth, as we
Must sift through the chaos of our own brittle lives.

A Tunnel in Tennessee

Here are places I have never been before: Tennessee, South Carolina,
Georgia—walking the ridge line between each I think of the breeches in earth
Leading to these lines, craters opening and making borders,

Separating each from the other, distinct—a map guides my way, yet every day
Of hiking I think about the Appalachian trail and how it came to be—I think of
My midlife years and how I want to make the most of each, a

Second chance given back to me by the mystery of what cannot be, of what we
Do not know, of what we can, in fact, never know—all we can do is peer through
A chink in an arched tunnel on a rainy day in May and marvel at

All that is already here anyway, step-by-step, day-by-day, each by each.

The Greening of the Willows

Every winter, my mom used to say, "wait, just wait, until the willows start to
Green"—she would begin to recite this litany deep into the darkness of
February—and one day, just like that, she would pronounce the greenness

Had returned and so, spring could not be far away—her own birthday, in early
March—often marked the beginning of a new season for her—and now I watch
The willows myself, waiting for them to green—and I want to

Tell her how green they are today, even though it is still raining, and chilly
Sometimes—this is now the second spring without her and I am often reminded
Of how she planned to live far into the summer, far past the

Winter she despised; instead, she died during the lingering chilly days of
January—I think of how she refused to talk about her own death, as if by
Pretending that word didn't exist then she would always live, forever—

I am reminded of how she wouldn't say which funeral home she wished to
"Make her Arrangements," she shuddered at the phrase—I think it frightened
Her to think of leaving this earth, of leaving me behind her—and

I wish I could tell her that I am alright, that I miss her everyday, but that I am
Okay—that is the hardest thing about losing someone close to you, not being
Able to talk to them about ordinary things, like the willows greening

In the spring—she still surprises me, in death, as in life—today I finally called
The New Yorker to explain I really no longer needed to receive two issues a
Month, mine and hers, a task I had been avoiding—I inquired how

Long her subscription ran for, how long she had planned to live—and I
Discovered that her magazine would be arriving for two more years—I smiled
At this evidence of her optimism made concrete—hope trumping

Fear—and I wanted to tell her that I was enjoying reading her copy every week,
Seeing her name on the address label reminded me of her, of how many times
We had sat together in April, watching the willows green.

Yellow Tulips

"If you fear something long enough, you will eventually make it happen,"
—Sylvia Plath

My mother was most afraid of knowing she was dying, of being alone, I was
With her, holding her; I was most afraid of my husband having an affair—as it
Turns out, he had

More than I'll ever be able to count—I was afraid of the embarrassment and
Shame of getting divorced—I was not prepared to be screamed at in court—I
Was terrified of

Being on my own, all alone, as I was when my mother died—perhaps it is that
The deepest, darkest fears we fight are what keep us most alive.

My daughter placed a bouquet of yellow tulips on her grandmother's grave.

October, The Champs-Élysées

I had an ominous sense on that sunny autumn afternoon as we strolled along
The Champs-Élysées, I handed my heart to you then, as you had repeatedly
Asked me to do; not then, but later, you proceeded to tear it to shreds, as I
Feared you might—and to see you through all the years,
Expecting, hoping you would love me, yet somehow feeling you would not,
Left me sorrowful, but clear; when the end came I knew I could never live with
You again: I requested an order from the court to remove you from our house.

Castanea: Flowering Chestnut Tree

Tonight, rain trickles down my roof—earlier today, I passed a chestnut tree
Burst into full bloom—I snapped a photograph just before the gloomy skies
Opened and let their gray opacity fall to earth; I stopped for awhile to

Admire this tree, this English chesten nut, from the old French *Chastain*—and
I remembered all the mornings when my father would drive me to school—he
Kept a watch over one of his particular favorite flowering

Trees, except he called it the candelabra tree—it would be May, and he would be
Waiting for the hanging buds to open—I couldn't understand all his enthusiasm
About the tree—but now I have a little better idea of what

Standing still admiring something that is beautiful can mean—we talked about
Everything on those rides—about why he believed in civil rights for everyone,
Why he feared organized groups and the hatred they could

Produce, why he disagreed with my mom about the protests against the
Vietnam War, what the body count meant, and why even one was too many—
Those trips were windows into his world, I now realize, journeys

Where he tried to impart to me everything he believed of importance—he was
Forty-six at my birth, and I know he worried about leaving me too early—
Miraculously, he stayed here on earth long enough to witness the

Birth of two of his three grandchildren, and I like to think somehow he knows
About the third—like the chestnut tree, he lived in many different lands, and he
Traveled the world—he liked to collect obscure nuggets of

Knowledge—when he went to Istanbul, he remarked there were chestnut trees
There too, except they were called Kestaneci—once he explained to me they
Symbolized chastity—most poignant, perhaps, is what he did not

Tell me: chestnut trees are not self-compatible; to pollinate, they need another
Tree, that fact reminds me of the New England tradition of planting a husband
Tree and a wife tree in the front garden, for symmetry and for

Solidity; much more important than the fact that roasted chestnuts are

Considered a delicacy on Saint Simon's Day in Tuscany is the idea that my Father and mother were two trees grown together, intertwined by their love.

Feeding America

My mom grew up hungry, no wonder she gave money to every charitable cause
She could—and now, I recognize the envelopes that come to my house
Addressed to her—as though she were still here—and I open them as though
I were her and she were still living, as if I could turn to her and ask how much
She was thinking of giving this year, or how she was feeling or tell her about her
Favorite writers—Mavis Gallant, Seamus Heaney, and Maxine Kumin—who
Have all died since last January—since I find myself saying often, since she died,
Since the last time we had a conversation, just a week before she died—and
Sometimes in the later afternoon, I still start to dial her number; I have to stop
Myself to remember that she really is no longer here. Sometimes I still listen to
The last confused voicemail she left me that I cannot bear to delete, the one
Where she kept asking me where I was, wondering if I could call her back soon
Because she had something important to tell me: I never got the chance to find
Out just what might have been on her mind; when I arrived in her quiet single
Room for the last time one Friday morning late in January, her eyes were closed.

Lilacs, May

Sometimes it's hard to remember how continuous life is—how one season
Bleeds into the next, how somehow, no matter what happens, the sun comes up
And the moon rises on another night and day—like this one Saturday in

May when friends came together from so far away and we all recall how it feels
To have warm wind brush against our bare legs, how the hot sun's rays catch
Our faces, how we laugh as we walk along the East river, how the city

Has changed since I used to come here to visit my grandmother, how friends
Have not changed, how we have each grown more like ourselves, as my father
Once famously proclaimed—and, in the end, what matters is that we

Each have the chance to become who we want to be—as tenuous as the lilac
Blossoms this May, as hopeful as the tendrils curl around our fingers, as jaunty
As the fragrant purple blooms tipping towards us, spilling out of a clear

Glass vase filled with water, tending towards us with hope, joy, and life.

Free Form Jazz

For my youngest

Something I did not understand before I had children: they teach you more
Than you teach them. From my youngest I have learned how to laugh a lot
More than I used to, how to roll with things when they don't go as planned
Which is, in fact,

More often than not, how to work hard and then play hard too—how to stop
Avoiding things I do not want to do—how to look around and decide whether
Something is worth worrying about or not—mostly not, especially if that

Something is something that definitely will not kill you—I have learned how to
Plan less and let a day take shape as it may—how to let the little things go—how
To see life more as an art than a science—how to laugh at and also to be kind to

Myself, for the first time, and that may be just the most important lesson.

White Rose

I think about those maps, everywhere now, that tell you where you are, on
Paper, screen, and machines that speak to us and say "you are here"—

Sometimes I wonder just where that here might be—it is so easy to get lost
Really, though we protest against our ignorance of not knowing where we

Are—my father used to tell me never to hold the map upside down, never to
Turn true north around—for him, that would have been a clear sign of

Incompetency—I think about staring at something for so long that we no
Longer know what it is—just the way we sometimes write one word over

And over again until it becomes squiggles before our eyes, nonsense in our
Brains—and in any single day a zillion images pass before me and, almost

Always there is one I keep seeing, even after I close my eyes—today, a single
White rose captured me, pulling me into soft velvet cloth petals just sprung.

Oia

Sometimes it is difficult to find a place of peace in our restless world; sometimes
It is hard to stop the noise from coming in, the ceaseless notifications of this
Or of that—sometimes it is almost impossible just to be—apparently, it keeps
Becoming more difficult to be quiet, relaxed—maybe when people

Find healing in quiet streams or sweet springs they found just that—even
When they were riding along in bumpy Surrey buggies or horses or climbing
Mountains looking for views—maybe they knew something we did not—to

Take the time to look at what is right in front of you, right before your very eyes.

Thunderstorm

In Pennsylvania the skies can open fast and let out gallons of rain on what was,
At least at the start, a very sunny day—I learned early here that not to carry an
Umbrella everywhere meant being soaked early and often—it is a certain kind

Blackness, the skies are big and wide here and it does not take much to hear a
Roll of thunder off the mountains and a flash of lightening before the dousing
Begins—just yesterday, the skies roared and I remember how afraid I used to be

Of thunder—how my dad would hold me and comfort me in the very middle
Of the night when I awakened, terrified—he would tell me not to worry, that
It was just the noise of the gods bowling in the skies—these many years later
I chuckle a

Bit over both the sweetness and the irony of his explanation—he certainly did
Not believe in God and, at least to my knowledge, he never went bowling.

Heather Corbally Bryant (formerly Heather Bryant Jordan) teaches in the Writing Program at Wellesley College. Previously, she taught at the Pennsylvania State University, the University of Michigan, and Harvard College where she won awards for her teaching. She received her A.B. with honors in History and Literature from Harvard where she received the Boston Ruskin Prize for her thesis, "Sight and Sensibility: A Study of Praeterita." She received her PhD in Modern British and Irish Literature from the University of Michigan where she was a Regents Fellow.

Her academic publications include, *How Will the Heart Endure: Elizabeth Bowen* and *the Landscape of War"* (University of Michigan Press, 1992). This study of the relationship between war and literature was awarded the Donald Murphy Prize for best first book. In addition, she has assisted in the research for the Cornell Yeats Series as well as publishing articles on Bowen, Yeats, O'Faolain, and T.S. Eliot. She has given papers at international conferences and was a plenary speaker at the centennial celebration of Elizabeth Bowen held at University College, Cork.

Beyond her academic publications, Heather Corbally Bryant has published a novel, *Through Your Hands* (2011) which received an Editor's Choice and Rising Star designation. The Finishing Line Press published her first poetry chapbook, *Cheap Grace,* in 2011. In addition, she has published poems in *The Christian Science Monitor* and the 2007 anthology of poetry, *In Other Words.* The Parallel Press Poetry Series of the University of Wisconsin Libraries published *Lottery Ticket,* her second chapbook in 2013. She has given readings at The Pennsylvania State University, The University of Wisconsin at Madison, The University of Illinois at Chicago, Southern Florida University in Ft. Lauderdale, Folio Bookstore, San Francisco the Palmer Art Museum in State College, the Transatlantic Connections Conference in Donegal, Ireland, Wellesley College, Notre Dame, Georgia State, and Harvard College, among other venues. *Compass Rose,* her third poetry collection, from The Finishing Line Press appeared in March 2016. Her first full-length collection of poetry, *My Wedding Dress,* was published by Finishing Line Press in the fall of 2016. *Eve's Lament,* her sixth poetry collection, is forthcoming from the Finishing Line Press in 2018. Her latest novel, *You Can't Wrap Fire in Paper,* will be published by the Ardent Writer Press in January of 2018.

www.ingramcontent.com/pod-product-compliance
Lightning Source LLC
Chambersburg PA
CBHW021204090426
42740CB00008B/1225